The Virtuosic Performer

Book One

9 Exciting Late Elementary to Early Intermediate Piano Solos

Margaret Goldston

The Virtuosic Performer, Books 1 and 2 were written for piano students who enjoy "showing off" their talents at recitals, competitions and festivals. Book 1 is for late elementary to early intermediate pianists. Book 2 is for intermediate to late intermediate pianists. These virtuosic solos should be performed with energy, emotion, drama and finesse.

The technical patterns in the pieces help develop strength and dexterity of the fingers as well as evenness and clarity of tone. Analyzing the sequential patterns improves sight-reading skills and facilitates the learning and memorization of the pieces.

It was fun composing these lively solos, and I hope students will enjoy learning the music and will impress audiences with each performance.

Margaret Goldston

Alfred

Flamenco Dancer

Margaret Goldston

With a fiery spirit

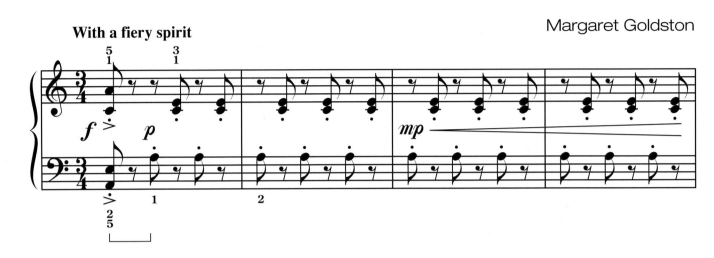

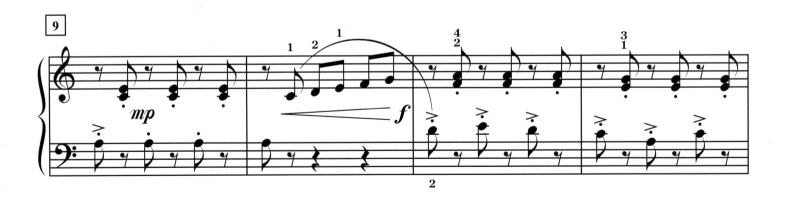

Expressively, slower

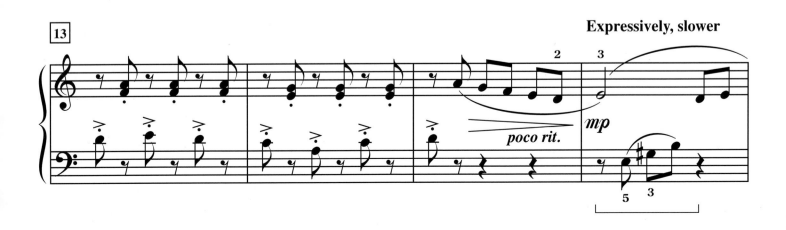

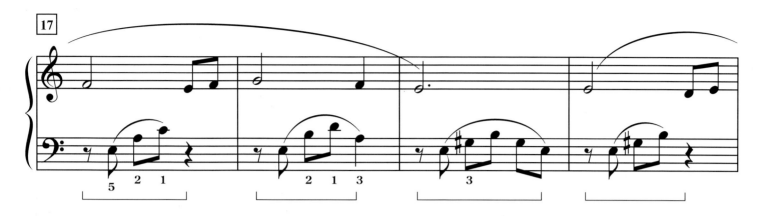

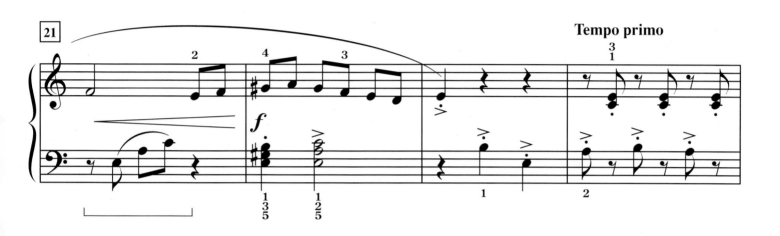

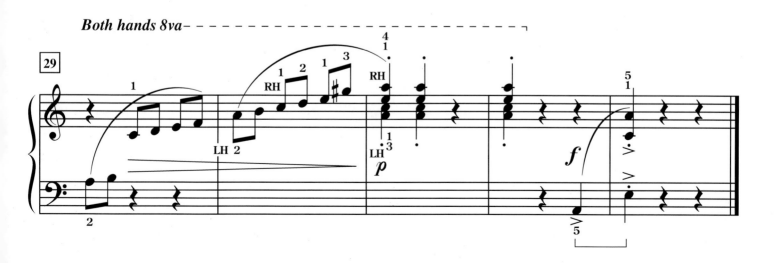

Taxi Toccata

Margaret Goldston

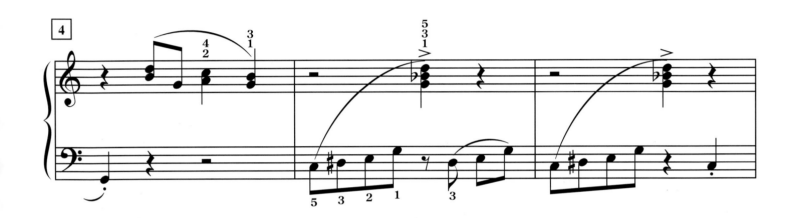

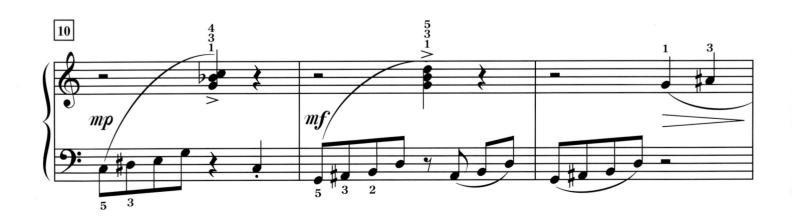

Arabesque

Margaret Goldston

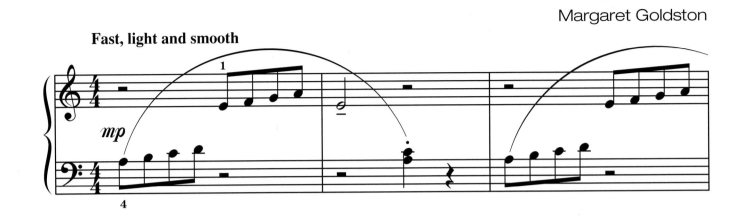

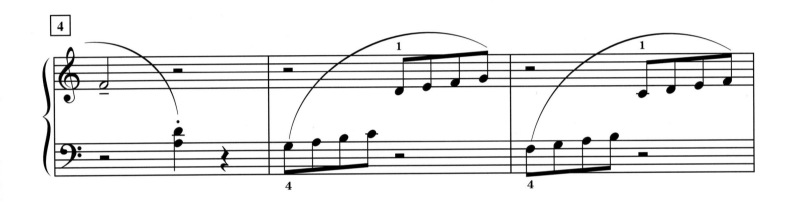

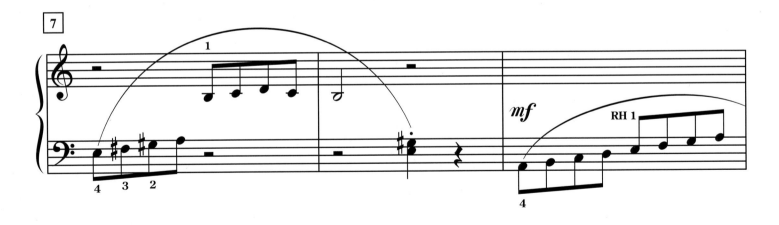

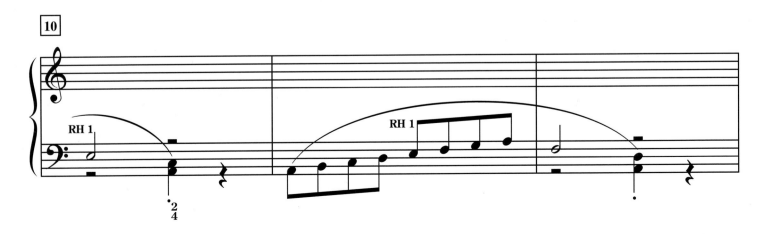

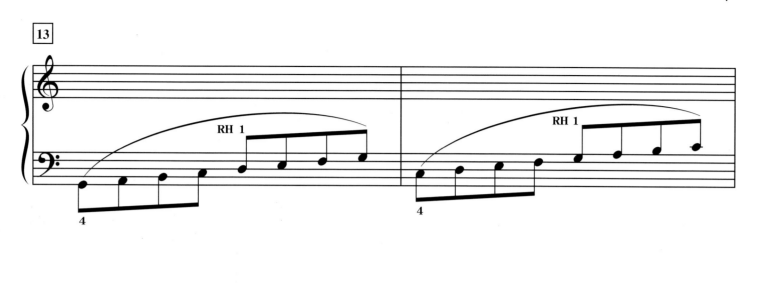

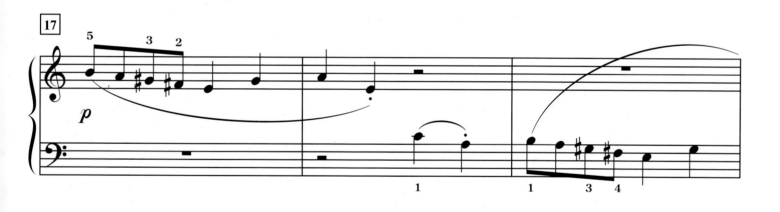

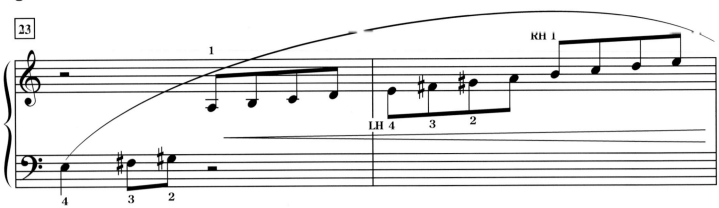
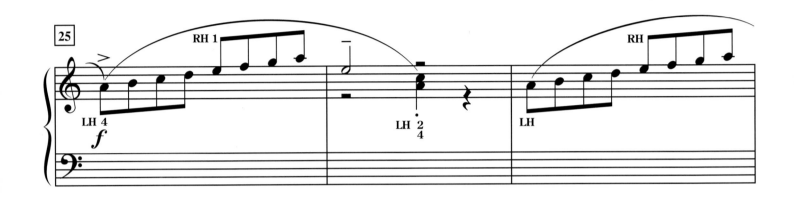

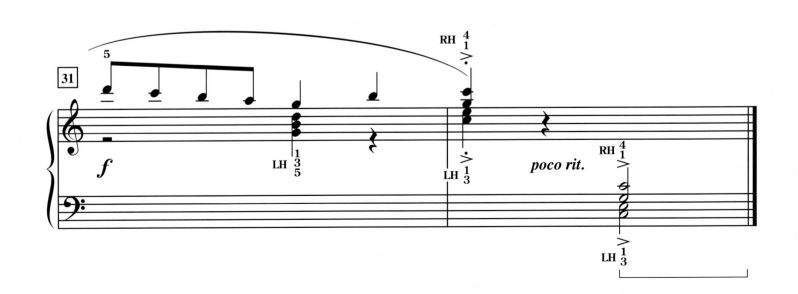

The Sparkling Brook

Rushing and melodious

Margaret Goldston

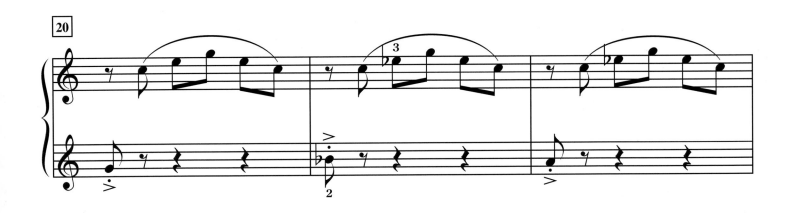

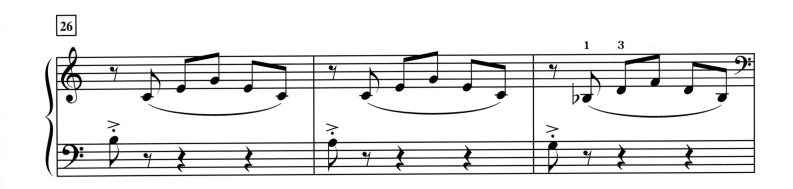

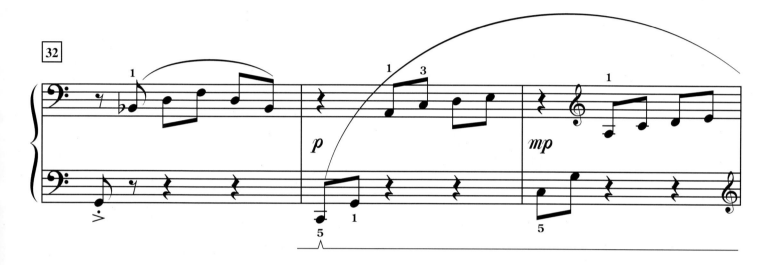

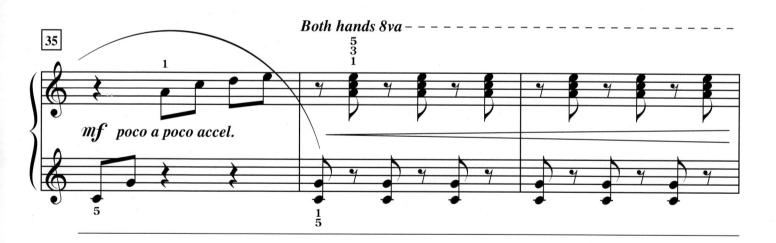

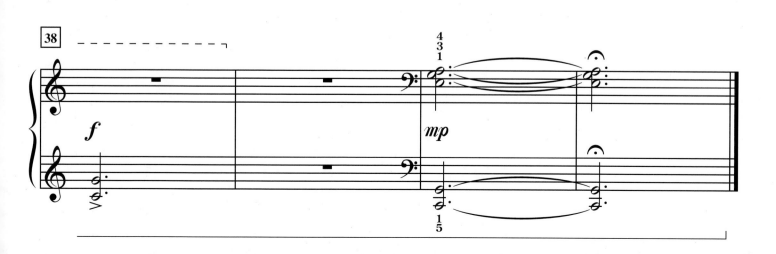

The Bold Cossacks

Margaret Goldston

Daring, with great energy

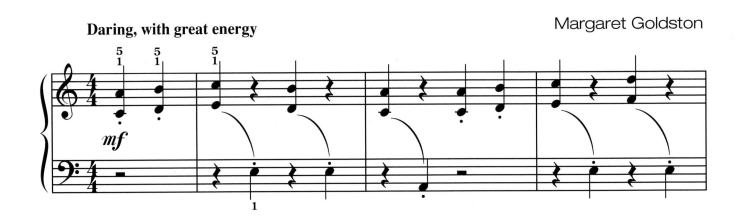

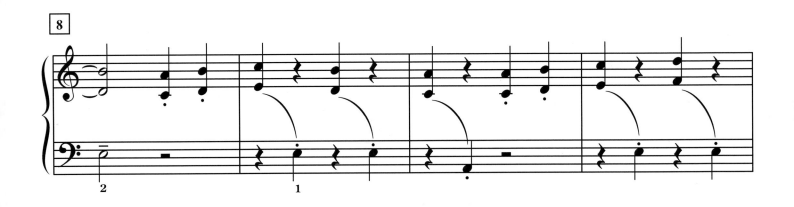

Chromatic Rag

Brightly, moderately fast

Margaret Goldston

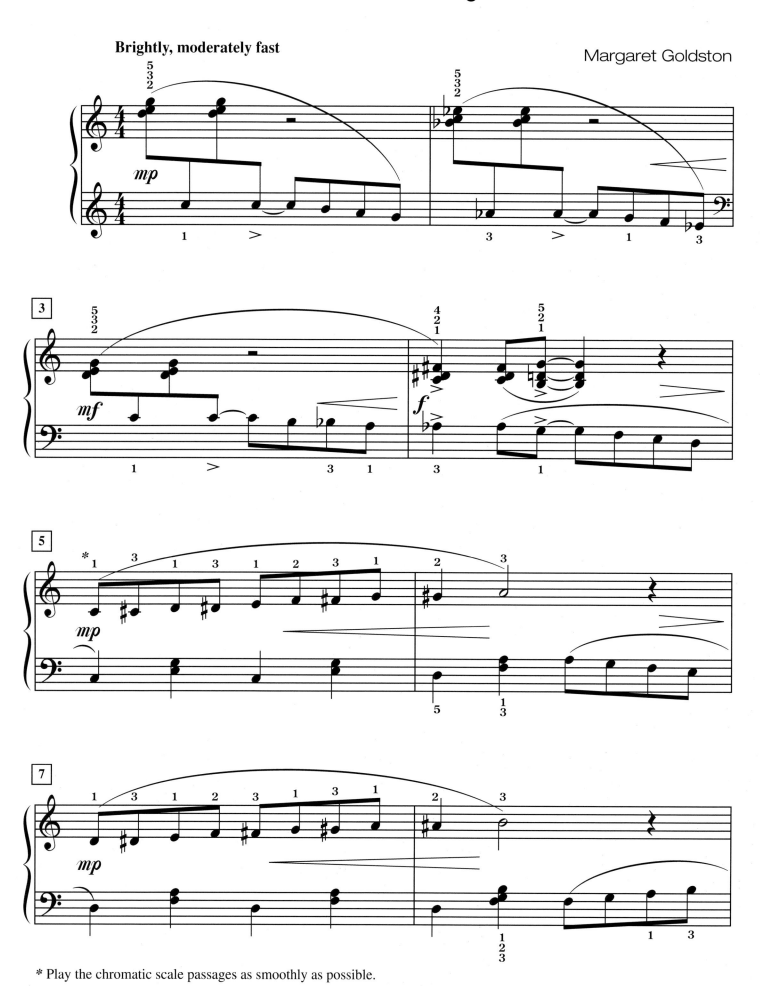

* Play the chromatic scale passages as smoothly as possible.

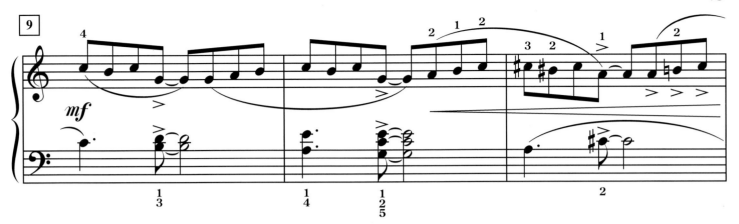

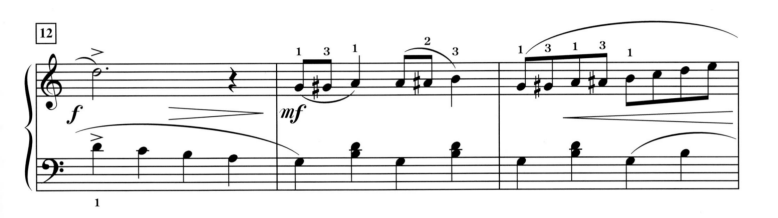

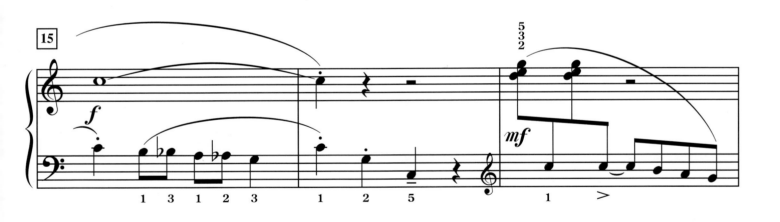

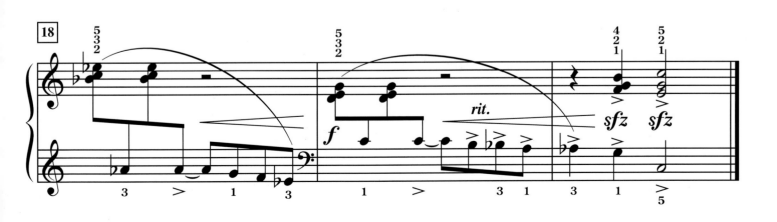

Gypsy Festival

Moderately, with feeling

Margaret Goldston

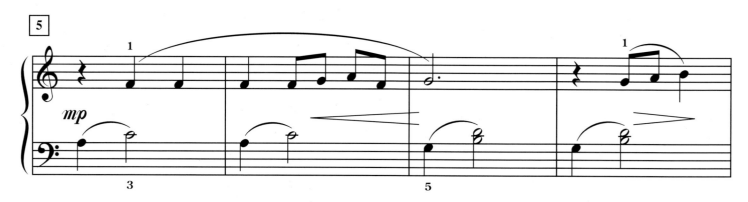

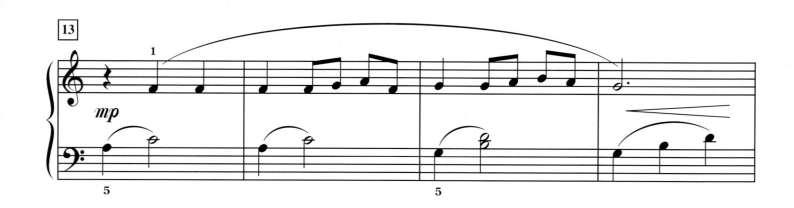

A little faster and more lively

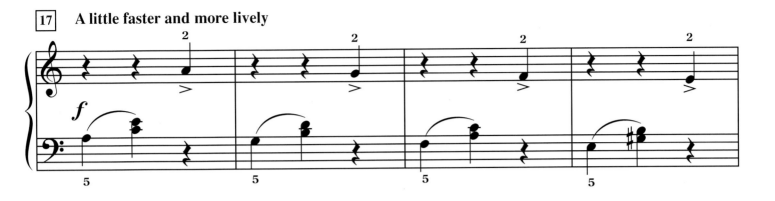

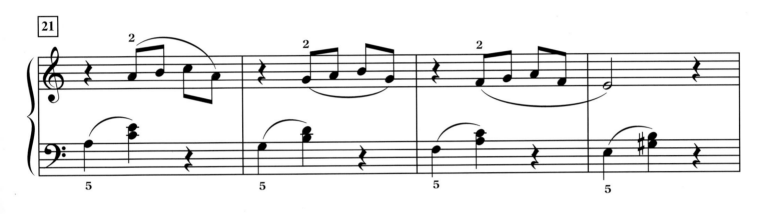

Both hands 8va

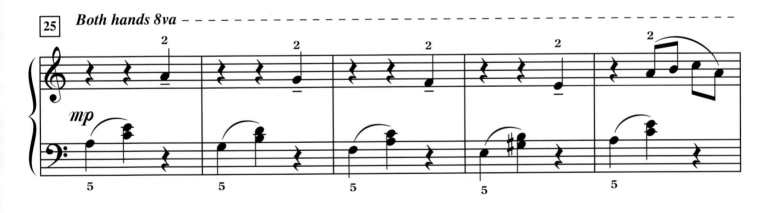

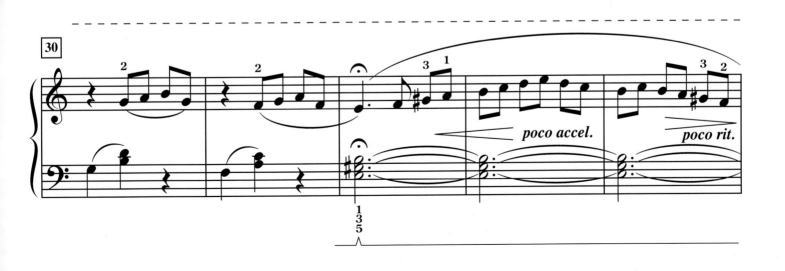

Exotic Adventure

Margaret Goldston

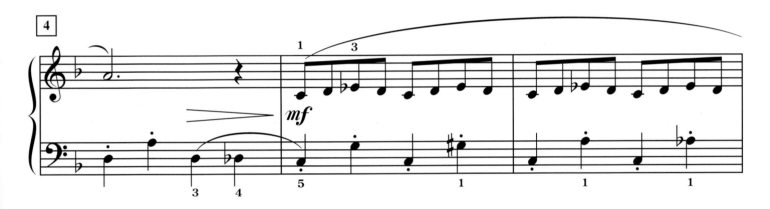

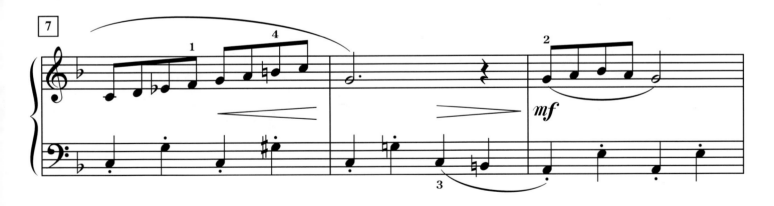

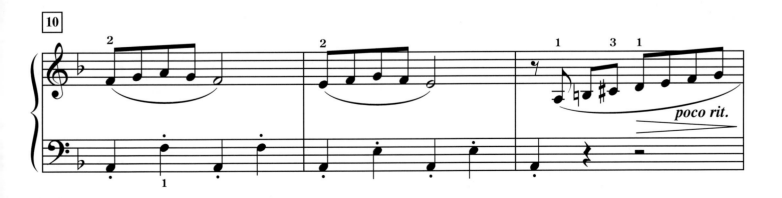

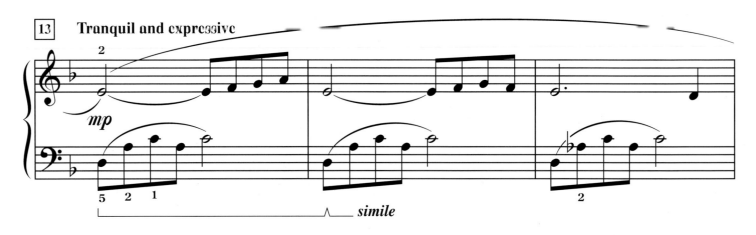

13 **Tranquil and expressive**

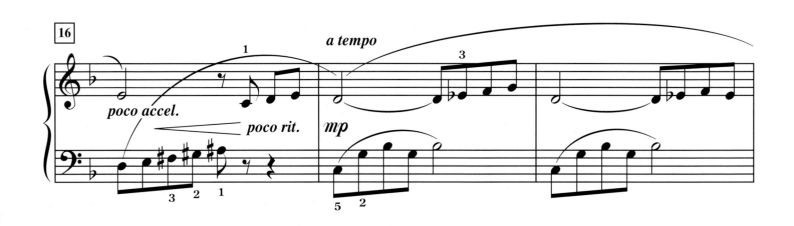

16

19

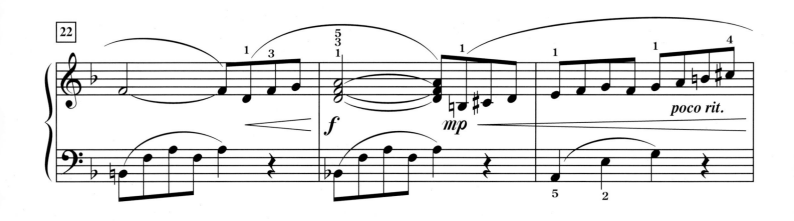

22

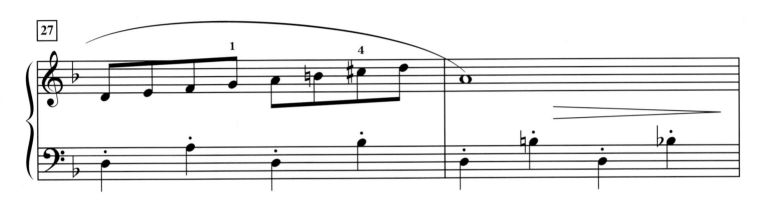

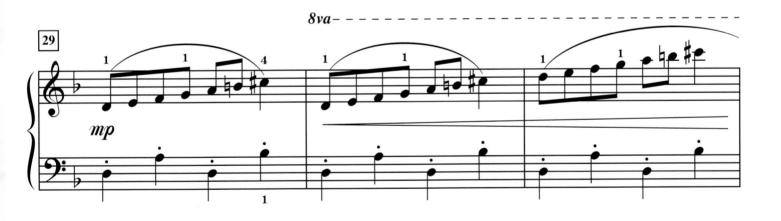

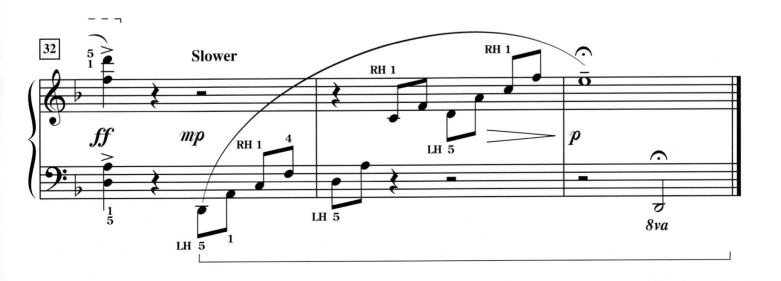

Runaway Train

Margaret Goldston

Fast, with a steady drive

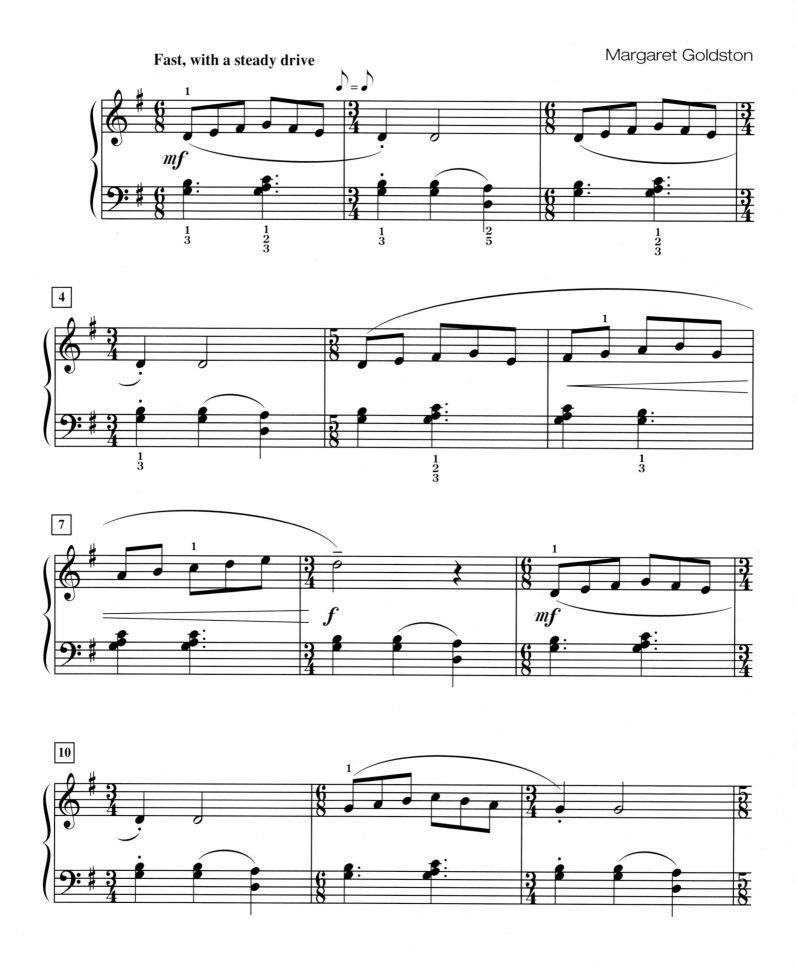

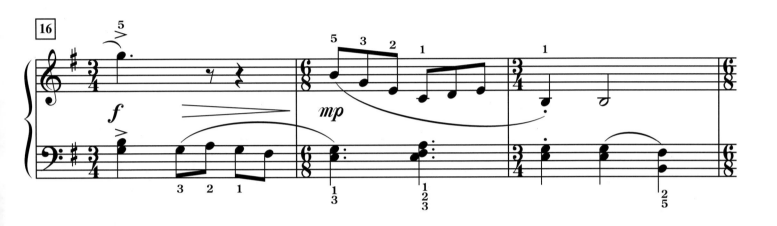

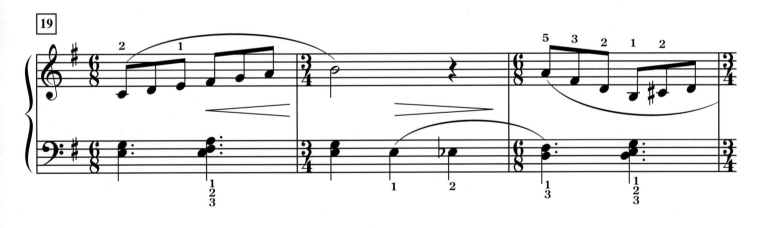

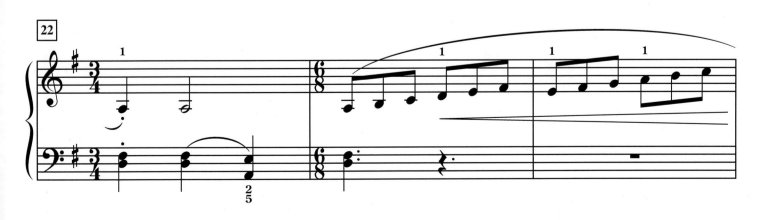

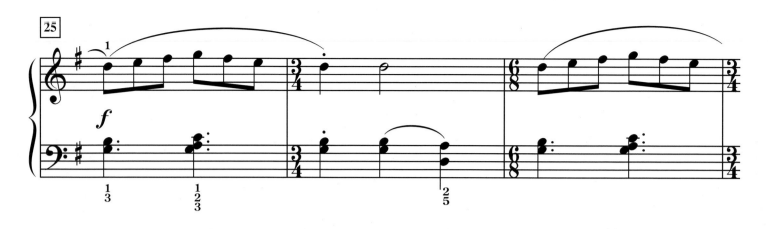

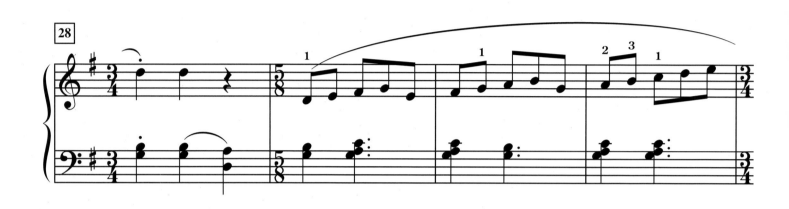

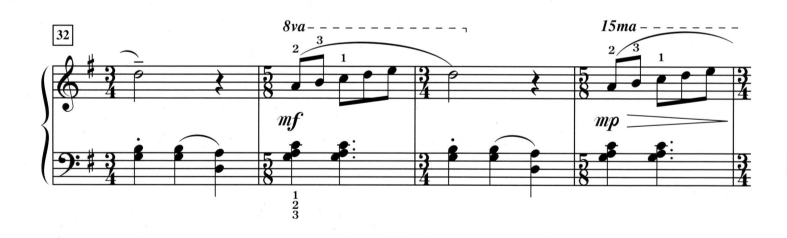